Environmental Education Materials: Guidelines for Excellence

NAAEE
NORTH AMERICAN
ASSOCIATION FOR
ENVIRONMENTAL
EDUCATION

North American Association
for Environmental Education

This book represents another in a series of documents published by NAAEE as part of the National Project for Excellence in Environmental Education.

Members of the Guidelines Writing Team

Deborah Simmons	Department of Teacher Education, Northern Illinois University, DeKalb, Illinois
Michele Archie	Harbinger Institute, Kapa'au, Hawaii
Terry Bedell	The Clorox Company, Oakland, California
Judy Braus	World Wildlife Fund—U.S., Washington, D.C.
Glenda Holmes	Washington, D.C. School District, Washington, D.C.
Mary Paden	Academy for Educational Development/GreenCom, Washington, D.C.
Robert Raze	Florida Gulf Coast University, Tallahasse, Florida
Andrew Smith	The American Forum for Global Education, New York, New York
Talbert Spence	Cranbrook Institute of Science, Bloomfield Hills, Michigan
George Walker	Office of Environmental Education, U.S. Environmental Protection Agency, Washington, D.C.
Brenda Weiser	Environmental Institute of Houston, University of Houston—Clear Lake, Houston, Texas

Special thanks to the hundreds of teachers, curriculum developers, educational administrators, environmental education specialists, and environmental scientists who have reviewed drafts of this document, and to Mary Vymetal-Taylor, Project Assistant for the National Project for Excellence in Environmental Education.

This project has been funded by the United States Environmental Protection Agency's Office of Environmental Education.

The contents of this document do not necessarily reflect the views and policies of EPA nor does mention of trade names or commercial products constitute endorsement or recommendation for use.

Additional funding and support for this project has been received from the Environmental Education and Training Partnership (EETAP), Northern Illinois University, the National Consortium for Environmental Education and Training (NCEET), World Wildlife Fund, World Resources Institute, National Fish and Wildlife Foundation, and the National Environmental Education and Training Foundation.

Additional copies of this book can be obtained from the NAAEE Publications and Membership Office, 410 Tarvin Road, Rock Spring, GA 30739, USA. Phone: (706) 764-2926. Fax: (706) 764-2094. E-mail: csmith409@aol.com Web site: www.naaee.org

ISBN 1-884008-41-0

TABLE OF CONTENTS

Introduction. 1

How to Use the Guidelines 3

Key Characteristic #1
      FAIRNESS AND ACCURACY 5

Key Characteristic #2
      DEPTH 7

Key Characteristic #3
      EMPHASIS ON SKILLS BUILDING 9

Key Characteristic #4
      ACTION ORIENTATION. 12

Key Characteristic #5
      INSTRUCTIONAL SOUNDNESS 14

Key Characteristic #6
      USABILITY 20

Glossary of Key Terms 22

INTRODUCTION

Environmental Education Materials: Guidelines for Excellence is a set of recommendations for developing and selecting environmental education materials. These guidelines aim to help developers of activity guides, lesson plans, and other instructional materials produce high quality products and to provide educators with a tool to evaluate the wide array of available environmental education materials.

These guidelines are grounded in a common understanding of effective environmental education. For many environmental educators, that understanding is rooted in two founding documents of the field: the *Belgrade Charter* (UNESCO-UNEP, 1976) and the *Tbilisi Declaration* (UNESCO, 1978).

The *Belgrade Charter* was adopted by a United Nations conference, and provides a widely accepted goal statement for environmental education:

> *The goal of environmental education is to develop a world population that is aware of and concerned about, the environment and its associated problems, and which has the knowledge, skills, attitudes, motivations, and commitment to work individually and collectively toward solutions of current problems and the prevention of new ones.*

A few years later, at the world's first intergovernmental conference on environmental education, the *Tbilisi Declaration* was adopted. This declaration built on the *Belgrade Charter* and established three broad objectives for environmental education. These objectives provide the foundation for much of what has been done in the field since 1978:

- To foster clear awareness of and concern about economic, social, political, and ecological interdependence in urban and rural areas;

- To provide every person with opportunities to acquire the knowledge, values, attitudes, commitment, and skills needed to protect and improve the environment;

- To create new patterns of behavior of individuals, groups, and society as a whole towards the environment.

As the field has evolved, these principles have been researched, critiqued, revisited, and expanded. They still stand as a strong foundation for a shared view of the core concepts and skills that environmentally literate citizens need. Since 1978, bodies such as the Brundtland Commission (Brundtland, 1987), the United Nations Conference on Environment and Development in Rio (UNCED, 1992), and the U.S. President's Council on Sustainable Development have influenced the work of many environmental educators.

Environmental Education and Learning

Environmental education is good education. Environmental education is learner-centered, providing students with opportunities to construct their own understandings through hands-on, minds-on investigations. Learners are engaged in direct experiences and are challenged to use higher-order thinking skills. Environmental education supports the development of an active learning community where learners share ideas and expertise, and prompt continued inquiry. Environmental education provides real-world contexts and issues from which concepts and skills can he learned.

Environmental education recognizes the importance of viewing the environment within the context of human influences, incorporating an examination of economics, culture, political structure, and social equity as well as natural processes and systems. As conceived in this document, the goal of environmental education is to develop an environmentally literate citizenry. Through comprehensive, cohesive programs, learners explore how feelings, experiences, attitudes, and perceptions influence environmental issues. They become knowledgeable about natural processes and systems and gain an understanding of human processes and systems. Learners are able to investigate and analyze environmental problems and issues using a variety of techniques. They also use basic science and math skills and explore the nature of bias. They develop a sense of their rights and responsibilities as citizens, are able to understand the ideals, principles, and practices of citizenship in our democratic republic, and they gain the skills necessary for citizenship.

A knowledgeable, skilled, and active citizenry is a key to resolving the environmental issues that promise to become increasingly important into the next century. While our schools play a major role, cultivating environmental literacy is a task that neither begins nor ends with formal education. Many parts of our society shape attitudes toward and knowledge about the environment—family, peers, religion, community, interest groups, government, the media, etc.

Environmental education often begins close to home, encouraging learners to understand and forge connections with their immediate surroundings. The awareness, knowledge, and skills needed for these local connections and understandings provide a basis for moving out into larger systems, broader issues, and a more sophisticated comprehension of causes, connections, and consequences.

Environmental education fosters skills and habits that people can use throughout their lives to understand and act on environmental issues. It emphasizes critical and creative thinking skills along with other higher level thinking processes that are key to identifying, investigating, and analyzing issues, and formulating and evaluating alternative solutions. Environmental education builds the capacity of learners to work individually as well as cooperatively to improve environmental conditions.

For each environmental issue there is not just one right answer or solution—there are many perspectives and much uncertainty. Environmental education cultivates the ability to recognize uncertainty, envision alternative scenarios, and adapt to changing conditions and information.

Knowledge, skills, and habits of mind translate into a citizenry that is better able to address its common problems and create advantage of opportunities, whether environmental concerns are involved or not.

Through the National Project for Excellence in Environmental Education, the North American Association for Environmental Education (NAAEE) is taking the lead in establishing guidelines for the development of coherent, cogent, and comprehensive environmental education programs. These guidelines will also point the way toward using environmental education as a means for meeting the standards set by the traditional disciplines and providing students with opportunities for synthesizing knowledge and experience across disciplines. Good quality environmental education programs facilitate the teaching of science, civics, social studies, mathematics, geography, language arts, etc. It is hoped that these guidelines will help educators develop meaningful environmental education programs that integrate across and build upon the disciplines.

in an effort to assure that these *Guidelines for Excellence* do reflect a widely shared understanding of environmental education, they were developed by a "writing team" comprised of environmental education professionals from a variety of backgrounds and organizational affiliations. This team took on the challenge of turning ideas about quality into usable guidelines. In addition, drafts of these guidelines were circulated widely to over 1000 practitioners and scholars in the field (e.g., teachers, educational administrators, environmental scientists, and curriculum developers), and their comments were incorporated into successive revisions of the document.

References

Brundliand, G. H. (1989) Our Common Future: The World Commission on Environment and Development. N.Y.: Oxford University Press.

UNCED (1992) Agenda 21: Programme of Action for Sustainable Development. Rio Declaration on Environment and Development. N.Y.: United Nations.

UNESCO-UNEP (1976) The Belgrade Charter. *Connect*: UNESCO- UNEP *Environmental Education Newsletter*, Vol.1 (l) pp. 1-2.

UNESCO (1978) Final Report lntergovernmental Conference on Environmental Education. Organized by UNESCO in Cooperation with UNEP, Tbilisi, USSR, 14-26 October 1977, Paris: UNESCO ED/MD/49.

HOW TO USE THE GUIDELINES

Environmental Education Materials: Guidelines for Excellence points out six **key characteristics** of high quality environmental education materials. For each of these characteristics, there are listed some **guidelines** for environmental education materials to follow. Finally, each guideline is accompanied by several **indicators** listed under the heading, "What to Look For." These indicators suggest ways of gauging whether the materials being evaluated or developed follow the guidelines. They are simply clusters of attributes you might look for to help you figure out whether the characteristic is embodied in the materials you are reviewing or developing.

There is a glossary at the end of the *Guidelines*. Words that are defined in this glossary are underlined the first time they appear in the text. Also, certain of the indicators are marked with a ◆ symbol. (See example below.)

The *Guidelines For Excellence* can help the educator, administrator, curriculum designer, or materials developer evaluate the quality of environmental education materials. They provide direction while allowing flexibility to shape content, technique, and other aspects of instruction.

These guidelines offer a way of judging the relative merit of different materials, a standard to aim for in developing new materials, and a set of ideas about what a well-rounded environmental education curriculum might be like. It is not reasonable to expect that all environmental education materials will follow all of the guidelines. For example, a set of materials might not present differing viewpoints, as outlined in guideline 1.2. This shortcoming does not necessarily mean that the materials should not be used. An instructor could work them into a larger set of activities that explores different viewpoints and helps learners discern opinion and bias in individual presentations of the issue. In cases such as this one, the *Guidelines for Excellence* can point out a weakness that instructors can compensate for in the way they use the materials.

Of course, no set of guidelines could be complete, and there are bound to be important characteristics missing. *Environmental Education Materials: Guidelines for Excellence* provides a foundation on which to build evaluation systems that work for different people in different situations. As a tool to inform judgment, these *Guidelines for Excellence* can contribute to more effective environmental education.

Sample format for the guidelines:

#1: Key Characteristic

   1.1) **Guideline**
      What to look for:
      • Indicator
      • Indicator
   1.2) ***Guideline***
      What to look for:
      • Indicator
      • Indicator
      ◆ Indicator

(Indicators marked with ◆ are accompanied by examples.)

Environmental Education Materials:
Guidelines for Excellence Summary

#1 Fairness and accuracy: EE materials should be fair and accurate in describing environmental problems, issues, and conditions, and in reflecting the diversity of perspectives on them.
    1.1 Factual accuracy
    1.2 Balanced presentation of differing viewpoints and theories.
    1.3 Openness to inquiry
    1.4 Reflection of diversity

#2 Depth: EE materials should foster awareness of the natural and build environment, an understanding of environmental concepts, conditions, and issues, and an awareness of the feelings, values, attitudes, and perceptions at the heart of environmental issues, as appropriate for different developmental levels.
    2.1 Awareness
    2.2 Focus on concepts
    2.3 Concepts in context
    2.4 Attention to different scales

#3 Emphasis on skills building: EE materials should build lifelong skills that enable learners to address environmental issues.
    3.1 Critical and creative thinking
    3.2 Applying skills to issues
    3.3 Action skills

#4 Action orientation: EE materials should promote civic responsibility, encouraging learners to use their knowledge, personal skills, and assessments of environmental issues as a basis for environmental problem solving and action.
    4.1 Sense of personal stake and responsibility
    4.2 Self-efficacy

#5 Instructional soundness: EE materials should rely on instructional techniques that create an effective learning environment.
    5.1 Learner-centered instruction
    5.2 Different ways of learning
    5.3 Connection to learners' everyday lives
    5.4 Expanded learning environment
    5.5 Interdisciplinary
    5.6 Goals and objectives
    5.7 Appropriateness for specific learning settings
    5.8 Assessment

#6 Usability: EE materials should be well designed and easy to use.
    6.1 Clarity and logic
    6.2 Easy to use
    6.3 Long-lived
    6.4 Adaptable
    6.5 Accompanied by instruction and support
    6.6 Make substantiated claims
    6.7 Fit with national, state, or local requirements

Environmental education materials should be fair and accurate in describing <u>environmental problems, issues,</u> and conditions, and in reflecting the diversity of perspectives on them.

1.1) Factual accuracy.
Environmental education materials should reflect sound theories and well-documented facts about subjects and issues.

What to look for:
• Sources of factual information are clearly referenced.

• Data are drawn from current and identified sources of information. (Knowing the source of information can aid in judging its trustworthiness or identifying possible bias.)

◆ Factual information is presented in language appropriate for education rather than for propagandizing.

• Information comes from primary sources-which provide context, documentation, and explanation - rather than from reviews or newspaper articles that simply provide bits and pieces of arguments or evidence.

• A range of experts in the appropriate fields reviewed the materials or participated in their development in another way. The materials provide a list of the people involved in development and review, and their areas of expertise.

1.2) Balanced presentation of differing viewpoints and theories.
Where there are differences of opinion or competing scientific explanations, the range of perspectives should be presented in a balanced way.

Example: 1.1

Pro and Con: Consumptive and Non-Consumptive Uses of Wildlife

The background information for this activity-intended for use with secondary school learners-is presented in language appropriate for education, rather than for propagandizing.

Consumptive uses are generally considered to be those in which wildlife is killed, as in hunting, fishing, and trapping. Such uses may include as a food source; for sport; for recreation; as a source of products for personal use; as a source of products for commercial use and sale; as a means to control damage to private land and crops; and as a population management tool.

Non-consumptive uses are generally considered to be those in which any wildlife is watched, studied, or recorded without being killed, such as in hiking, birdwatching, sketching, and photography. Such uses may be for purposes of recreation, education, and research. Some non-consumptive uses may actually be vicarious, such as movie, television, and gallery viewing of wildlife.

Just as consumptive uses of wildlife have impacts on individuals and populations, so can non-consumptive uses. There are times, for example, when non-consumptive uses may actually be damaging to wildlife and its habitat, such as observation of wildlife at too close ranges during breeding seasons, and high human use of areas where endangered species may be negatively impacted.

Project WILD Activity Guide. Council for Environmental Education. Reprinted with permission from Project Wild, © 1983, 1985, 1992.

What to look for:
• Proponents of differing viewpoints reviewed the materials or helped develop them in another way. The materials list the people involved in development and review, and their organizational affiliation.

• Opinions or policies of an agency or organization are clearly identified.

- Scientifically and socially credible positions and explanations are covered thoroughly, while other positions are also mentioned. (Balanced presentation does not mean giving equal time and space to every opinion or perspective, but treating major positions fairly.)

- Materials communicate areas of consensus among scientists or other experts.

1.3) Openness to inquiry.
Materials should encourage learners to explore different perspectives and form their own opinions.

What to look for:

- Educators are given tools to use in helping learners to form and express opinions about competing theories.

◆ Exercises are suggested for helping learners explore personal and societal values and conflicting points of view within the context of the issue.

- Materials encourage an atmosphere of respect for different opinions and an openness to new ideas.

- There are exercises that encourage learners to understand the opinions of their peers.

- Materials suggest projects that encourage learners to collect and analyze their own data and to compare those data to similar data from other places.

- Activities encourage learners to become discerning readers and observers of media coverage of environmental matters.

1.4) Reflection of diversity.
Different cultures, races, genders, social groups, ages, etc., are included with respect and equity.

What to look for:

- Materials contain descriptions and illustrations that depict people of various races, ethnic groups, genders, and social groups in a respectful and equitable manner.

Example: 1.3

What Do People Think?

This activity shows an openness to inquiry, suggesting ways for students of all ages to explore values and conflicting points of view.

Procedure

1. Tell the children that they are going to be responsible for creating a survey to find out other people's knowledge and attitudes about food and hunger.

2. Go around the room and ask each student to contribute possible questions for the survey.

3. Have the group choose a list of eight to fifteen questions to be used in the survey [depending on their age].

4. Type or carefully write out the survey.

5. Distribute the surveys. Have each person fill one out. Compare the results.

6. Ask the children to take two or three surveys home and find people in their neighborhoods of any age to answer the questions. Ask that they bring the surveys back to class.

7. When the surveys are returned, compile the results.

8. Discuss how people's attitudes differ or are the same, how attitudes of community members differ from attitudes of group members, how well-informed people seem to be, whether there are any attitudes that the children would like to change, and how these could be changed.

9. Journals—Give children time to put their surveys in their journals and to make entries about what other community members think about food and hunger and on what they've learned about doing a survey.

Rubin, Laurie. *Food First Curriculum*, Oakland, CA: Institute for Food and Development Policy, 1984

- Where such variety is appropriate, the content and illustrations depict rural, suburban, and urban settings.

- If the material is designed for nationwide use, the content and illustrations reflect geographic differences appropriately.

- Experts in multicultural education and members of historically under-represented groups, such as women and people of color, have been involved in the development and review process.

- Readings and additional resources that present concepts and perspectives from different cultures are offered.

KEY CHARACTERISTIC #2 DEPTH

Environmental education materials should foster awareness of the natural and built environment, an understanding of environmental <u>concepts</u>, conditions, and issues, and an awareness of the feelings, values, attitudes, and perceptions at the heart of environmental issues, as appropriate for different <u>developmental</u> levels.

2.1) Awareness. Materials should acknowledge that feelings, experiences, and attitudes shape environmental perceptions and issues.

What to look for:

• As appropriate for the developmental level, opportunities are provided for learners to explore the world around them.

• Activities provide opportunities for experiences that increase learners' awareness of the natural and built environments.

• Materials help learners understand the interdependence of all life forms and the dependence of human life on the resources of the planet and on a healthful environment.

• Exercises and activities encourage students to identify and express their own positions regarding environmental issues.

2.2) Focus on concepts. Rather than presenting a series of facts, materials should use unifying themes and important concepts.

What to look for:

• Concepts from environmental sciences fields such as ecology, earth science, chemistry, conservation biology, etc., are presented, as appropriate for the intended developmental level.

• Concepts from social sciences fields such as economics, anthropology, sociology, and political science are presented, as appropriate for the intended developmental level.

• Facts are presented—and vocabulary words introduced and defined—in context and support of the important concepts.

• Ideas are presented logically and are connected throughout the materials, emphasizing a depth of understanding rather than encyclopedic breadth.

◆ Materials include a clearly articulated <u>conceptual framework</u> that states the concepts to be learned and relates them to each other.

2.3) Concepts in context. Environmental concepts should be set in a context that includes social and economic as well as ecological aspects.

What to look for:

• Environmental issues are explained in terms of specific concepts.

• Historical, ethical, cultural, geographic, economic, and sociopolitical relationships are addressed, as appropriate.

• Learners are offered opportunities to examine multiple perspectives on the issue and to gain an understanding of the complexity of issues, as appropriate for their developmental level.

• Further investigations help learners probe more deeply into the ecological, social, and economic aspects of issues, and their interrelationships.

• Concepts are introduced through experiences relevant to learners' lives.

• Materials help learners to make connections among the concepts.

• Learning is based on students constructing knowledge through research, discussion, and application to gain conceptual understanding.

2.4) Attention to different scales. Environmental issues should be explored using a variety of scales as appropriate, such as short to long time spans, localized to global effects, and local to international community levels.

What to look for:

• Materials consider communities of different scales. These scales include the local, regional, national, and global levels.

Example: 2.2

Project Learning Tree Pre K-8 Activity Guide: Conceptual Framework

The PLT conceptual framework links concepts from different fields around common themes such as diversity, systems, and patterns of change.

Theme: Diversity

Throughout the world, there is a great diversity of habitats, organisms, societies, technologies, and cultures.

Diversity in Environments

1.1 Biological diversity results from the interaction of living and nonliving environmental components such as air, water, climate, and geologic features.

1.2 Forests, as well as other ecosystems, contain numerous habitats that support diverse populations of organisms.

1.3 The Earth's atmosphere, water, soil, climate, and geology vary from region to region, thus creating a wide diversity of biological communities.

Diversity of Resources and Technologies

2.1 Humans use tools and technologies to adapt and alter environments and resources to meet their physical, social, and cultural needs.

2.2 Technologies vary from simple hand tools to large-scale and complex machinery, mechanisms, and systems.

2.3 Successful technologies are those that are appropriate to the efficient and sustainable use of resources, and to the preservation and enhancement of environmental quality.

Diversity Among and Within Societies and Cultures

3.1 Human societies vary ... and inhabit many land forms and climates [around] the world.

3.2 Humans ... create differing social, cultural, and economic systems and organizations to meet their physical and spiritual needs.

3.3 The standard of living of various peoples ... depend[s] on ... the availability, utilization, and distribution of resources; the government; and culture of its inhabitants.

3.4 Natural beauty ... enhances the quality of human life by providing artistic and spiritual inspiration, as well as recreational and intellectual opportunities.

---

*Project Learning Tree Pre K-8 Activity Guide.*Washington, DC:American Forest Foundation, 1996.

• Linkages are clear among communities of all levels.

• Local, regional, continental, and global geographic scales are used to help learners understand that issues can be important, widespread, and complex.

• Materials examine issues over a variety of temporal scales so that short-term and long-term problems, actions, and impacts are clear.

KEY CHARACTERISTIC #3 EMPHASIS ON SKILLS BUILDING

Environmental education materials should build lifelong skills that enable learners to address environmental issues.

3.1) Critical and <u>creative thinking</u>. Learners should be challenged to use and improve their <u>critical thinking</u> and creative skills.

What to look for:

● Materials offer learners opportunities to practice critical thinking processes such as problem definition, forming hypotheses, collecting and organizing information, analyzing information, synthesizing, drawing conclusions, formulating possible solutions, and identifying opportunities for action.

● Materials encourage learners to practice creative thinking processes such as modeling, using metaphors and analogies, and formulating questions.

● Learners are challenged to use higher level thinking processes such as identifying bias, inferring, relating, applying, and reflecting.

● Materials provide guidance for judging the validity of various sources of information, and learners are encouraged to apply these guidelines.

● Learners are given opportunities to practice these skills individually and in groups.

3.2) Applying skills to issues. Students should learn to arrive at their own conclusions about what needs to be done based on thorough research and study, rather than being taught that a certain course of action is best.

What to look for:

● Materials help students learn to identify, define, and evaluate issues on the basis of evidence and different perspectives. Ethical and value considerations are included.

● Materials provide a list of organizations and other resources that learners can use to explore the issue on their own, as appropriate for their developmental level. This list should include groups and resources with various perspectives.

● There are opportunities to use different methods of evaluating environmental issues and their potential solutions, as appropriate for the intended age level. These methods may include <u>risk analysis</u>, <u>cost/benefit analysis</u>, ethical analysis, environmental impact analysis, analysis of <u>cumulative effects</u>, different kinds of economic analyses, social impact analysis, etc. Materials help learners understand the strengths, weaknesses, and biases of these different means of evaluating an issue.

● Learners are encouraged to develop their own solutions to issues.

● Environmental issues are presented with a range of possible solutions as well as information about how the problems are currently being addressed. Materials compel learners to consider the implications of different approaches.

3.3) Action skills. Learners should gain basic skills needed to participate in resolving environmental issues.

What to look for:

◆ Materials give learners an opportunity to learn basic skills for addressing environmental issues, as appropriate for the intended age level. These skills may include defining an issue, determining if action is warranted, identifying others involved in the issue, selecting appropriate action strategies and understanding their likely consequences, creating an action plan, evaluating an action plan, implementing an action plan, and evaluating results.

• Learners are challenged to hone their ability to forecast and to plan for the long term.

• Learners are encouraged to practice interpersonal and communication skills, including oral and written communication, group cooperation, leadership, conflict resolution, and others.

◆ Learners are provided with opportunities to develop a variety of citizenship skills, including participation in the political or regulatory process, consumer action, using the media, and community service.

• Materials and activities help students sharpen basic laboratory and field skills such as experimental design, observation, data collection, and data analysis.

• Materials encourage students to learn basic skills of applied science, including environmental monitoring, evaluating others' research, and setting up an independent research proposal.

• Learners are instructed in the use of various forms of technology that help them develop and apply their skills. These technologies might include computers and electronic communication networks, data gathering equipment, video equipment, etc.

Example: 3.3
Investigating and Evaluating Environmental Issues and Actions:
Skill Development Modules

This program offers learners opportunities to learn basic skills for addressing environmental issues and to develop a variety of citizenship skills.

Program Description

This program consists of a series of six illustrated modules. These modules are designed to provide training in both the investigation and action skills needed by a responsible citizen. The program is highly interdisciplinary and introduces students to environmental issues, the skills needed to investigate and evaluate issues, the skills needed for information processing, and those skills used by responsible citizens in applying environmental action strategies.

Key Activities

Chapter I: Environmental Problem Solving.
• Students explore the impact of beliefs and values on environmental issues.
• Students critically analyze environmental issues.

Chapter II: Getting Started on Issue Investigation.
• Students identify environmental issues.
• Students learn how to write research questions.
• Students learn how to gain information from secondary sources.
• Students compare and evaluate information sources.

Chapter III: Using Surveys, Questionnaires, and Opinionnaires in Environmental Investigations.
• Students learn how to draw samples from human populations.
• Students learn how to gain information using primary sources.
• Students collect and record data using model surveys, questionnaires, and/or opinionnaires.

Chapter IV: Interpreting Data from Investigations.
• Students learn how to draw conclusions, make inferences, and formulate recommendations.
• Students learn how to communicate data using a number of strategies including graphs.

Chapter V: Investigating an Environmental Issue.
• Students select and investigate environmental issues.

Chapter VI: Environmental Action Strategies.
• Students learn six methods of citizenship action.
• Students analyze the effectiveness of individual versus group action.
• Students evaluate the action decisions of others.
• Students develop and evaluate action plans of their own.

Hungerford, H., Litherland, R., Peyton, R.B., Ramsey, J. & Volk, T. *Investigating and Evaluating Environmental Issues and Actions: Skill Development Modules.* Champaign, IL: Stipes Publishing Company, 1996.

KEY CHARACTERISTIC #4 ACTION ORIENTATION

Environmental education materials should promote civic responsibility, encouraging learners to use their knowledge, personal skills, and assessments of environmental issues as a basis for environmental problem solving and action.

4.1) Sense of personal stake and responsibility. Materials should encourage learners to examine the possible consequences of their behaviors on the environment and evaluate choices they can make which may help resolve environmental issues.

What to look for:
• Materials promote <u>intergenerational</u> and <u>global responsibility</u>, linking historical and current actions with future and distant consequences.

• Learners are provided with opportunities to reflect on the effects of their actions and to sort out their opinions about what, if anything, they should do differently.

• Materials contain examples of people of different ages, races, genders, cultures, and education and income levels who have made a difference by taking responsible action.

• Materials convey the idea that many individual actions have cumulative effects, both in creating and addressing environmental issues.

4.2) <u>Self-efficacy</u>. Materials should aim to strengthen learners' perception of their ability to influence the outcome of a situation.

What to look for:
• Materials challenge learners to apply their thinking and act on their conclusions.

◆ Materials include a variety of individual and community strategies for citizen involvement and provide learners with opportunities to practice these strategies through projects they generate individually in their school or in the larger community.

• There are examples of successful individual and collective actions. Learners are encouraged to examine what made these actions successful. (Where actions were not successful, students are encouraged to examine the reasons for failure.)

• Learners are encouraged to share the results of their actions with peers and other interested people.

Example: 4.2
Different Kinds of Action

Following are some examples of individual and community strategies for citizen involvement included in environmental education materials. The actions range in scale from the individual level to the larger community level.

How Can I Help? In this activity, students are encouraged to take action to improve their community by making some positive environmental changes. Students brainstorm a list of possible projects, narrow the list to ones that particularly interest them, and select one or more that can be accomplished during the school year. Simple projects might include picking up litter from an area; planting flowers, grass, shrubs, or trees; scrubbing graffiti off walls; or designing a mural for a nearby wall.

Ecological Citizenship: Urban Environmental Education and Action. Chicago, IL: The Chicago Academy of Sciences, 1996.

Pollution Detectives This activity encourages students to seek out and describe water quality in their community. Students may choose to develop a photo essay or videotape to accompany their presentation, and may wish to make presentations at a schoolwide assembly, a community meeting, or a meeting of a local environmental group.

Always a River. Cincinnati, OH: USEPA Office of Research and Development, 1991.

Car Trouble This lesson begins by asking students to examine their own use of motor vehicles [in light of] facts about motor vehicle usage. Students then examine the hidden environmental costs of driving ... and look back at the automobile's history to see how our dependence on the gasoline-powered automobile developed. Finally, students consider what they can do to address the problems outlined in the lesson.

Paden, M., ed. *Teacher's Guide to World Resources.* Washington, DC: World Resources Institute, 1994.

KEY CHARACTERISTIC #5 INSTRUCTIONAL SOUNDNESS

Environmental education materials should rely on instructional techniques that create an effective learning environment.

5.1) <u>Learner-centered instruction</u>. When appropriate, learning should he based on learner interest and on the learner's ability to <u>construct knowledge</u> to gain conceptual understanding.

What to look for:
• Activities allow learners to build from previous knowledge and lead toward further learning.

• Learners gain understanding through research, discussion, application, and practical experiences.

• Instruction encourages learners to undertake their own inquiry.

• Where appropriate, activities and projects use learner questions and concerns as a starting point.

• Materials encourage learner participation in planning and assessing learning. Materials encourage learner reflection on the process and content of learning.

5.2) Different ways of learning. Materials should offer opportunities for different modes of teaching and learning.

What to look for:
• Materials encourage educators to experiment with a range of instructional methods to reach learners with a variety of <u>learning styles</u>. These techniques may include research, experimentation, observation, lecture, discussion, creative expression, field studies, role playing, independent work, cooperative learning, cross-age teaching, etc.

◆ Important concepts are conveyed in several ways (visual, auditory, tactile, etc.) so that all students can understand them.

• Materials and activities are developmentally appropriate for the designated grade, yet sensitive to individual differences in educational experience and learning mode.

• Opportunities are provided for students to learn from expression and experience—for example, using music, art, poetry, and drama, or involving parents, families, and the community in learning activities.

• Diverse sensory involvement is a criterion for selecting learning activities.

• Learners are challenged to learn different skills that reflect their <u>multiple intelligences</u>.

• Learning is accessible to students with limited English proficiency.

5.3) Connection to learners' everyday lives. Materials should present information and ideas in a way that is relevant to learners.

What to look for:
• Concepts to be taught are related directly to students' experiences.

• Case studies and examples are relevant to the learner. If the material is designed for use in a specific area of the country, the content and illustrations are appropriate for that area.

• Instructional materials are easy for students to use and understand.

• The content and associated activities are presented in a way that encourages students to have enjoyable learning experiences.

• Materials provide for continuing involvement throughout the year by the learner, both at home and at school. Means for involving learners' families or care givers are suggested.

Example: 5.2
Aqua Words

This activity, intended for use with primary and intermediate grade levels, illustrates how concepts can be conveyed in more than one way within one activity. Its objective is to enable students to describe a variety of ways and reasons why water is important to people and wildlife.

Procedure

1. Have the students bring in photographs from magazines that show water. Ask them to look especially for pictures that show how living things depend on water. Display these photographs and use them as a basis for discussion.

2. Ask students to think about some of the ways they have used water that day. Emphasize how all living things are ultimately connected to water.

3. Using a long strip of butcher paper or spacious empty chalkboard for recording, ask the students to list at least 100 words that have something to do with water. *Note: For younger students, use pictures or a combination of words and pictures.*

4. Using the list of words that were recorded, ask the students to create word trees of water-related words. Begin with a simple word tree [and move to] more complex ones.

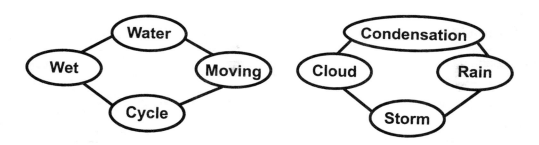

5. When students have finished several word trees, have them look at what they have done and create one or two poetic definitions of water or water-related concepts. These could begin: "Water . . ." or "Water is . . ." If not definitions, the students could create sentences or even paragraphs about water.

6. Have students write their poetic statements onto various shades of blue, aqua, gray, white, and green construction paper cut to graphically fit the feeling of their idea.

Aquatic Project WILD, Council for Environmental Education. Reprinted with permission from Project WILD,© 1987, 1992.

5.4) Expanded learning environment.

Students should learn in environments that extend beyond the boundaries of the classroom.

What to look for:

◆ Students learn in a diverse environment which includes the school yard, laboratory, field settings, community, and other settings beyond the classroom.

◆ Learners are encouraged to share their knowledge and their work with others.

• Materials use examples that reflect real-world experiences.

• Materials suggest partnerships with local civic organizations, businesses, religious communities, or governments to explore a local issue.

• Partnerships with local universities, colleges, or technical schools are encouraged to allow learners to participate in research, environmental monitoring, creative projects, etc.

◆ Materials suggest experiential learning activities in which students immerse themselves in an activity outside the classroom—tracking a wild animal, for example, or interviewing different sides in a community controversy.

• Materials suggest linkages to informal, experiential, and service learning opportunities in the community.

• Lists of written materials and other resources for further study are included.

Example: 5.4
Streams

Studying a local stream can include activities that immerse learners in experiences outside of the classroom and encourage them to share their knowledge.

Study a Stream

Divide the children into small groups and give each group a Stream Studies sheet to complete during their explorations. Put needed equipment in a central spot. Send half the groups to a slow part of the stream and half to a fast-moving section. When Stream Study sheets are complete, compare results:

* What is the bottom like where the water is moving fast? slow?

* Where were the most animals found?

* How are animals different in fast and slow sections of the stream?

Follow-up Activity

History of a Local Stream Have the children interview local residents or read in old newspapers about the history of a local stream (uses, floods, bridges, pollution) and write an article for the newspaper.

Lingelbach J., ed. *Hands On Nature.* Woodstock, VT: Vermont Institute of Natural Science, 1986.

5.5) Interdisciplinary.

The materials should recognize the interdisciplinary nature of environmental education.

What to look for:

◆ Materials clearly list the subject disciplines integrated into each lesson or lessons, suggest tie-ins with other subject areas, such as the science disciplines, social studies, math, geography, English, arts, physical education, occupational education, etc.

• The material helps develop skills useful in other subject areas, such as reading comprehension, math, writing, and map reading and analysis.

• Where appropriate, materials are keyed to national standards for other disciplines or standards adopted by the school district or state.

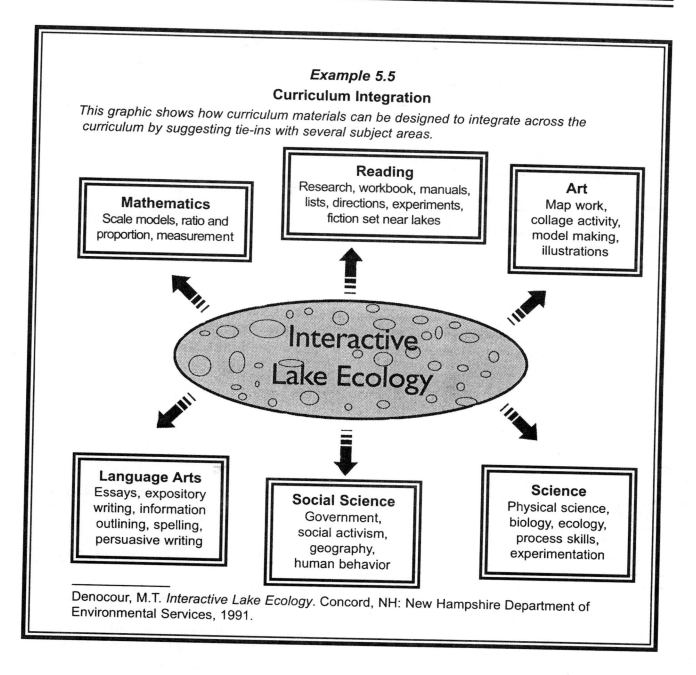

Example 5.5
Curriculum Integration

This graphic shows how curriculum materials can be designed to integrate across the curriculum by suggesting tie-ins with several subject areas.

Reading
Research, workbook, manuals, lists, directions, experiments, fiction set near lakes

Mathematics
Scale models, ratio and proportion, measurement

Art
Map work, collage activity, model making, illustrations

Interactive Lake Ecology

Language Arts
Essays, expository writing, information outlining, spelling, persuasive writing

Social Science
Government, social activism, geography, human behavior

Science
Physical science, biology, ecology, process skills, experimentation

Denocour, M.T. *Interactive Lake Ecology*. Concord, NH: New Hampshire Department of Environmental Services, 1991.

5.6) Goals and objectives. Goals and objectives for the materials should be clearly spelled out.

What to look for:

• Goals and objectives for <u>learner outcomes</u> are clearly stated.

• The content is appropriate for achieving the objectives, and steps for accomplishing the objectives are identified in written lesson or activity plans.

• Instructional methods are appropriate to the guide's goals.

• Objectives should be in keeping with goals and objectives of general education.

5.7) Appropriateness for specific learning

settings. Claims about the material's appropriateness for the targeted grade level(s) and the implementation of the activity should be consistent with the experience of educators.

What to look for:

• The content is appropriate (level and language) for the target grade levels. The examples, terminology, and comparisons used are within the probable vocabulary and experience of students.

• Lesson-related activities can be accomplished in the time specified, with resources available.

• Experiments and activities appear to be relevant, accurate, predictable, and suitable for the target grade levels. Materials include suggestions for appropriate variations and extensions.

• Activities are efficient. The amount of time required is consistent with the importance of what is to be learned.

• Environmental responsibility is modeled in the design, underlying philosophy, and suggested activities of the lessons and materials.

5.8) Assessment. A variety of means for assessing learner progress should be included in the materials.
What to look for:
◆ Materials state expected learner outcomes and provide examples of how to use specific performance-based assessments such as portfolios, open-ended questions, group or independent research, or other appropriate projects to indicate mastery.

◆ Learner outcomes are tied to the goals and objectives.

• Means of assessing learners' baseline understandings, skills, and concepts at the beginning of each lesson are included.

• Materials use current educational assessment techniques.

• Suggested assessment techniques are practical and efficient.

• Assessment is on-going and tied to student learning.

• Expectations are made clear to students at the onset of an activity.

• Students are encouraged to assess their own and other students' work.

Example: 5.8
Irrigation Interpretation
This activity, designed for upper elementary and middle school, states learner objectives in measurable terms and provides specific performance-based assessments to indicate mastery.

Objectives
Students will:

• identify reasons people irrigate.

• construct a classroom irrigation system and monitor crop growth.

• describe different irrigation methods and evaluate the costs and benefits of each.

• propose explanations for an ancient culture abandoning its homeland.

Assessment
Have students:

• demonstrate and identify irrigation systems (Part I, steps 3-6).

• construct classroom irrigation models, demonstrating and comparing different irrigation systems (Part II, steps 1 and 2).

• develop a questioning strategy to determine why a culture could abandon its homeland (Part III).

• create a chart summarizing irrigation techniques and assessing ecological and economic benefits and costs (Wrap Up).

Upon completing the activity, for further assessment, have students:

• research and identify on a world map locations with salinization problems.

• investigate and report on what is being done to overcome salinization problems.

Project WET *Curriculum and Activity Guide.* Bozeman, MT:The Watercourse and Houston, TX: Western Regional Environmental Education Council. 1995.

Example: 5.8
Sample Rubric

This rubric was developed by an Earth Systems teacher for use in evaluating individual student research projects.

Research Time Utilization	The student needed continual reminders to get back to work. Work may be inappropriate to the project.	The student was usually on task, but needed an occasional reminder to get back to work. All work is appropriate.	The student was always on task and did not need reminders to get back to work.
Participation In Project	The student does not add an equitable amount of work to the project and does not meet all requirements for the length of presentation.	The student adds an equitable amount of work to the project, but may not meet all requirements for the length of the presentation.	The student adds an equitable amount of work to the project and meets all requirements for the length of the project.
Accuracy of Information During Presentation	The student's information is lacking in content and is not factually correct in many places. Information may not be pertinent to the presentation.	The student's information is for the most part factually correct. Information may not be pertinent to the presentation.	The student's information is factually correct and pertinent to the presentation.
Clarity of Presentation	The student's work is not well planned. The student was confused by much of the information presented. The student was not clear in explaining topics.	The student's work is well planned. There seemed to be some confusion or misinterpretation of information.	The student's work is well planned and clearly explained. The student showed a clear command of the information presented.
Visual Aid Worksheet, or Simple Demonstration	The device used by the student was not used at a timely place in the presentation, had little bearing on the presentation, or was absent from the presentation.	The device used by the student was appropriate for the presentation. It may have been used in a more appropriate manner The design of the device may not have maximized the learning.	The use of the device was timely and appropriate. The design of the device was constructed to maximize learning.

Mayer, V.J. and Fortner, R. W. eds. *Science is a Study of Earth*, Columbus, OH: Ohio State University, 1995.

KEY CHARACTERISTIC #6 USABILITY

Environmental education materials should be well designed and easy to use.

6.1) Clarity and logic. The overall structure (purpose, direction, and logic of presentation) should be clear to educators and learners.

What to look for:

• Materials are clearly and engagingly written. Main concepts are well articulated. Examples in the text are appropriate to the content and easily understood.

• Instructions for educators are clear and concise.

• The following information is included in a straight forward manner:
   ❑ Intended audience/grade level;
   ❑ Instructional setting and optimal number of learners;
   ❑ Disciplines and concepts covered;
   ❑ Intended learner outcomes;
   ❑ Process skills addressed (i.e., observing, communicating, comparing, ordering, categorizing, relating, inferring, applying)
   ❑ Equipment needed;
   ❑ Safety precautions if appropriate;
   ❑ Time needed for activity;
   ❑ Brief overview of the activity;
   ❑ Instructions for conducting the activity;
   ❑ Suggestions for assessing the activity; and
   ❑ Pre- and post-activities, such as suggestions for enrichment activities, if appropriate.

• Background information for the educator is adequate and accurate, and there is a listing of additional resources.

• Materials are organized sequentially and in an easy-to-use fashion.

• Lab and field work, and other activities, are clearly linked to related content material.

6.2) Easy to use. Materials should be inviting and easy to use.

What to look for:

• The layout of materials is interesting and appealing for educators and learners.

• Illustrations, photographs, maps, graphs, and charts are useful, clear, and easy to read.

• The material is easy for educators to keep and use (8.5x 11", 3-hole punched, able to lie flat on desk).

• Masters for student handouts and overhead transparencies are easily duplicated.

• Copyright is spelled out or permission to copy is granted.

• Where appropriate, materials are available in electronic form such as computer file, CDROM, or over the Internet.

6.3) Long-lived. Materials should have a life span that extends beyond one use.

What to look for:

• Materials include information on where replacements, updates, equipment, and special supplies can be obtained.

• Equipment and materials are listed, reasonably accessible, inexpensive, and simple to use.

• Student materials are sufficiently supplied. Consumable instructional materials are of good quality and sufficient quantity to support the objectives.

• Nonconsumable materials can be reused by another educator.

6.4) Adaptable. Materials should be adaptable to a range of learning situations.

What to look for:

• Suggestions are provided for adapting lessons and activities for learners from particular ethnic or cultural backgrounds.

- Materials are available in more than one language, if appropriate.

- Where appropriate, the materials suggest easy adaptations for different environments, such as indoor and outdoor environments, formal and informal settings, large and small classes, mixed-level classes, or rural, suburban, and urban settings.

- There are suggestions for finding low-cost or no-cost alternatives for the equipment and materials needed.

- Materials provide suggestions for adaptations for students with special learning needs, language needs, and physical needs.

- Materials offer ideas for adapting to different grade levels.

6.5) Accompanied by instruction and support. Additional support and instruction should be provided to meet educators' needs.

What to look for:
- Professional development programs are accessible to educators in your area.

- Continuing technical support for educators is provided (for example, a toll-free telephone number or a list of local or regional points of contact for questions about the materials).

- Instructional programs provide follow-up activities or evaluations and help develop a network of practitioners.

- Materials include lists of essential resource and supporting materials, such as agency contacts, references to videos, information on computer databases, etc.

6.6) Make substantiated claims. Materials should accomplish what they claim to accomplish.

What to look for:
- Claims of learning outcomes are substantiated by systematic evaluation rather than merely by letters of endorsement and anecdotal comments from users.

◆ Materials were field tested under conditions similar to their intended use and evaluated in terms of stated goals and objectives prior to wide scale implementation.

Example: 6.6
Field Testing
This acknowledgments section indicates that new activities were field tested and evaluated.

Thank you to the following parents, teachers, naturalists, environmental educators and youth leaders who donated large amounts of their time and consideration as they field-tested and evaluated the activities newly designed for this book: (The list of 46 names includes many people involved in formal and nonformal education).

Caduto, M.J. and Burchac, J. *Keepers of Life.* Golden, CO: Fulcrum Publishing, 1994.

- If materials are part of a larger program, the program provides for continuous feedback and modification once it is underway.

- Educators who work in the settings in which the material is intended to be used participated on the development team or reviewed drafts of materials.

- Experts in learning theory, evaluation, and other appropriate educational disciplines were involved on the development team or reviewed drafts of materials.

6.7) Fit with national, state, or local requirements. Environmental education materials should fit within national, state, or local standards or curricula. (Also see guideline #5.5 for other ideas about fitting with local curricula.)

What to look for:
- Materials have been or could be easily correlated with national, state, or local requirements or learning objectives.

- Materials can be readily integrated into established curricula.

GLOSSARY OF KEY TERMS

Assessment. Measurement of a learner's achievement or progress.

Concept. A general idea or understanding, especially one based on common or related attributes of specific instances. For example, the concept of ecological interdependence—that all living elements of an ecological system depend on the others—is based on a knowledge of interrelationships among living things in many specific systems.

Conceptual framework. An organized sequence of ideas that directs teaching towards a focused understanding.

Constructing knowledge (constructivist learning). A guiding philosophy that believes that individuals make meaning of situations for themselves through a dynamic combination of knowledge they already possess, new knowledge presented to them, social interaction, and personal reflection and experience. This personally constructed knowledge by the learner evolves throughout the learner's lifetime. (See Cheek, D.W. (1992) *Thinking Constructively about Science, Technology, and Science Education.* SUNY Press.)

Cost/benefit analysis. An examination of a program that seeks to evaluate the resources expended in relation to the outcome, often noted in financial terms.

Creative thinking. Thinking which results in connections or possibilities previously unrecognized by or unknown to the learner.

Critical thinking. Analysis or consideration that relies on logical methods and deductive reasoning.

Cumulative effects analysis. A systematic process using as many known facts and factors as possible to estimate the total impact or likely result of many individual events or actions.

Developmental appropriateness. The suitability of an activity for learners of a certain age or cognitive ability.

Environmental issue. Related to, but distinguished from an environmental problem. An environmental issue reflects the presence of differing perspectives on possible solutions to an environmental problem.

Environmental monitoring. Systematic measurement, over time, of one or more indicators of an ecosystem's stability or health.

Environmental problem. Related to, but distinguished from, an environmental issue. An environmental problem results from an interaction between human activity and the environment.

Experiential learning. Learning by means of personal experience or direct observation.

Fact/factual information. A verifiable phenomenon or association. Factual information can be consistently corroborated by standardized means.

Global responsibility. A person's accountability for the potential or actual impact of individual actions on the earth and the world community.

Goal. A desired outcome from an activity.

Informal learning opportunities. Situations in which learning can occur without formal or traditional direction from an instructor.

Interdisciplinary. A knowledge view and curriculum approach that applies methodology and language from more than one discipline to examine a central theme, issue, or experience. Related terms include *multidisciplinary* (juxtaposing several disciplines focused on one problem with no direct attempt to integrate) and *transdisciplinary* (beyond the scope of the disciplines, for example starting with a problem and bringing to bear knowledge from relevant sources).

Intergenerational responsibility. A person's accountability for the potential or actual impact of individual actions on future populations.

Learner centered instruction. Instructional methods that are driven by the individual needs of the student rather than externally imposed goals or objectives.

Learner outcomes. The intended cognitive result of an educational program.

Learning styles. The belief that individuals favor particular methods of learning (e.g., oral vs. written, self-taught vs group mediated) and can optimize their understanding when such methods are available to them within the learning environment.

Multiple intelligences. Theory advanced by Howard Gardner (see *Multiple Intelligences*: The Theory in Practice. New York: Basic Books. 1993) that classifies cognitive abilities according to seven broadly grouped aptitudes: linguistic intelligence, logical-mathematical intelligence, spatial intelligence, bodily-kinesthetic intelligence, musical intelligence, interpersonal intelligence, and intrapersonal intelligence. In 1998, an 8th intelligence, the naturalistic intelligence, was added.

Objective. A statement of a specific measurable or observable result desired from an activity.

Risk analysis. Activity which seeks to predict the overall results or broad consequences and degree of impact, whether beneficial or not, of a given project or activity.

Rubric. A scoring mechanism for performance-based tests that provides model answers.

Self-efficacy. One's ability, or attitude about that ability, to be a catalyst or agent of change in one's own life and in situations involving others.

Service learning. Learning in which the student takes part in a project or activity that is beneficial to some segment of the community.

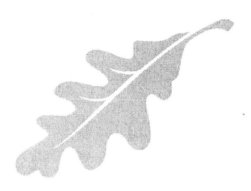